Pro Stock
Drag Racing

by Martin Hintz and Kate Hintz

CAPSTONE PRESS

MANKATO, MINNESOTA

C A P S T O N E   P R E S S

818 North Willow Street • Mankato, MN 56001

Printed in the United States of America.

Library of Congress Cataloging-in-Publication Data
Hintz, Martin.
    Pro stock drag racing/by Martin and Kate Hintz
    p. cm. -- (Drag racing)
    Includes bibliographical references and index.
    Summary: Describes the sport of pro stock racing and the vehicles and various people involved.
    ISBN 1-56065-388-4
    1. Drag racing--Juvenile literature. 2. Dragsters--Juvenile literature. [1. Drag racing.] I. Hintz, Kate. II. Title. III. Series: Drag racing (Mankato, Minn.)
GV1029.3.H55 1996
796.7'2--dc20

                                        96-22344
                                        CIP
                                        AC

Photo credits
Archive, 8. Mark Bruederle, 38. FPG/Jeffrey Sylvester, 26.
Don Gillespie, cover, 4, 6, 14, 18, 20, 24, 28, 30, 36, 41, 47.
Martin Hintz, 17, 22, 33. Steve Mohlenkamp, 11, 12, 34.

Table of Contents

Chapter 1 Pro Stocks 5

Chapter 2 History 9

Chapter 3 The Cars 13

Chapter 4 Safety 19

Chapter 5 The Drag Race 25

Chapter 6 A Driver's Life 35

Photo Diagram 36

Glossary 42

To Learn More 44

Useful Addresses 45

Internet Sites 46

Index 48

Words in **boldface** type in the text are defined
in the Glossary in the back of this book.

Chapter 1
Pro Stocks

Dragsters are cars made for quarter-mile (400 meter) racing. Pro stocks look like regular cars more than any other kind of professional dragster. Still, it is easy to see that pro stocks belong on a racetrack.

They have powerful engines and lightweight bodies. They have oversized tires. Most of them have huge **hood scoop**s.

Drag races are tests of **acceleration**. The cars start from a complete stop. Pro-stock dragsters reach speeds over 200 miles (320 kilometers) per hour. Top drivers can finish a race in about six seconds.

Pro stock dragsters race down a quarter-mile (400-meter) track.

Drivers

Drivers earn their racing licenses only after many hours of driving. They take tests to move through the different racing **classes**. Pro-stock drivers have to prove that they are good and safe long before they actually race.

Drag racing is a fast, exciting sport. Many people think it is fun to watch top drivers test their skills. Drivers try to match their best times whenever they race. Race fans like the speed and the roar of the cars.

Race fans like to watch drivers test their skills against each other.

Chapter 2
History

Drag racing started in Southern California in the 1930s. Drivers raced on city streets. They raced from stoplight to stoplight. Whoever made it to the end of the block first was the winner.

These early drag races were not very safe. There were many accidents.

Racers moved outside of town. They looked for straight, flat land. They raced on country roads, on abandoned airport runways, and in the desert.

Early drag racing took place on city streets.

Eventually, local racing clubs were organized. They established rules and safety standards.

The First Drag Race

The first organized drag race was held in 1950 in Santa Ana, California. The National Hot Rod Association (NHRA) was formed the next year. A man named Wally Parks started the NHRA. He is known as the father of modern drag racing.

The NHRA set the official length of a drag-racetrack at a quarter-mile (400 meters). A car could go all out in that distance without damaging its engine. Drivers could go very fast and still come to a safe stop.

The first national championship was held in 1954 in Great Bend, Kansas. Today, the NHRA **sanctions** races across the United States and Canada. Drivers know that sanctioned events will be safe and well run.

Pro stocks have gotten faster and faster over the years.

Faster and Faster

Over the years, pro stocks have gotten faster and faster. Fans were amazed when these dragsters reached 100 miles (160 kilometers) per hour. Eventually, even the 200-mile (320-kilometer) per-hour mark was passed.

Fans enjoy watching the pro stocks set new records. Nobody knows how high the speed record can go. Nearly every year, the dragsters go a little faster than the year before.

Chapter 3
The Cars

The body of a pro-stock car must be a body made for **production cars**. Many pro-stock bodies are made by Plymouth, Dodge, Ford, Chevrolet, and Chrysler. The body cannot have been built before 1968.

The company that makes the body must also make the engine. The **wheel base** must be the same as a production car. These are the reasons why a pro-stock dragster looks so much like a street car.

Pro stocks look so much like street cars because their bodies are the same as those made for production cars.

Modified

A pro stock can be **modified** to make it faster. Pro-stock bodies are dipped in acid. This decreases air resistance. It makes the cars faster.

All unnecessary equipment is removed from the interior of the car. There is no odometer to measure mileage. There is no fuel gauge and no radio. The hood and trunk are often made of plastic. There is only one seat for the driver. All these things make pro stocks lighter and faster.

Engines

Pro-stock engines burn racing gasoline. The gasoline and air are mixed inside the engine's cylinders. Spark plugs ignite the mixture. There is an explosion in the engine.

The explosion moves a piston inside a cylinder. There are several pistons and cylinders. The pistons connect to gears and shafts that make the wheels turn.

There are many ways to modify an engine. Hood scoops increase air flow to the engine.

Drivers have a tight fit inside of pro-stock cars.

Headers allow the exhaust to exit the engine quickly. All these changes increase an engine's power.

Tires

Pro-stock tires are called racing slicks. Because they have no tread, more rubber touches the track. This gives pro-stock cars better **traction**.

Many racers use wheels that are narrower than the tires. They do not put much air in the tires. When they go fast, the tires flatten out. This gives them even better traction.

Sometimes drivers put extra weight over the rear end. Some drivers use a car battery. Extra weight helps the tires grab the track.

Mechanics

Mechanics keep the cars in top racing shape. Mechanics are often called wrenches. Each car's team of mechanics is called a **pit** crew.

Race teams haul their equipment in semitrailers.

A semitrailer hauls the cars, the pit crews, and their tools from track to track. They even carry several back-up engines. Pit crews can replace or repair any part quickly.

Some fans get a pit pass. It allows them to hang out in the pit area. They can watch mechanics get a dragster ready to race. They can ask questions.

Chapter 4

Safety

Both cars and drivers must meet high safety standards. Each car is inspected by track officials. A team can enter the pits only when its dragster is approved.

Even the audience has to think about safety. Dragsters are very loud. Most fans wear earplugs so they do not damage their hearing. Drivers, mechanics, track workers, and safety crews wear earplugs, too.

Driver Safety

Each driver is buckled into a harness. In case of an accident, a latch releases the

Pro stocks are very loud. Most fans cover their ears or wear earplugs when these dragsters race.

harness. This allows the driver to escape easily. Harnesses are inspected and replaced often.

A **roll cage** surrounds the driver. If there is a crash, the roll cage keeps the car's roof from caving in. Windshields are made of **safety glass**. They do not break easily.

Each driver wears a helmet, a fire-resistant suit, a mask, goggles, and gloves. Many drivers wear straps that keep their arms from flopping outside the roll cage if their car rolls over.

The area at the end of the track is called the shutdown strip. This is where the cars slow down. A safety team is always on duty there. If a car's brakes fail, it runs into a sand trap at the edge of the track. The sand stops the car quickly.

Fuel and Oil

Fuel can leak from a car's tank if there is a crash. The fuel can burn or explode. Safety crews must get to the driver immediately.

Drivers wear helmets and are surrounded by roll cages.

Some safety crew members are professionals and some are volunteers.

The safety crew has fire extinguishers, axes, and crowbars. They have giant chain saws that can cut through metal. Sometimes they need a powerful tool called the jaws of life. The jaws of life can pry open a smashed car.

If oil or fuel is spilled on the track, a car could spin out of control. Safety crews clean up any spills. They use a piece of equipment called a track sweeper. A track sweeper is like a street sweeper.

The People in the Crew

Safety crews wear fire-resistant suits, heavy gloves, goggles, and helmets. Some safety-crew members are professional fire fighters who work part time at a track. Others are full-time professionals.

The NHRA safety team is known as the safety safari. They travel to events across North America. They make sure races, racers, and fans are safe and secure.

Ambulances are ready at all races. Medical teams are ready at both ends of the track. If a driver is injured, the ambulance rushes him or her to the hospital.

Serious injuries are rare at a drag race. But anything can happen. Safety crews are there just in case.

Chapter 5

The Drag Race

On race day, the cars gather in rows near the starting line. The rows are called staging lines. They are called forward when it is their turn to race. Two vehicles compete in each **heat**. Cars race in classes. This makes the races fair.

The Burnout Box

Workers pour water and chemicals under the rear tires of cars about to race. The drivers rev their engines. Their left feet are on the brakes. Their right feet are pushing the accelerator pedals.

Dragsters gather in staging lines while they wait to race.

The cars stand still, shaking while the tires spin. The drivers are burning oil and other **debris** off the rear tires to get better traction.

This process is done in an area that used to be called the bleach box. When drag racing first started, bleach was poured under the tires. But bleach often overheated and caused fires. Bleach is not allowed at most tracks today. People today call it a burnout box or water box instead of a bleach box.

Christmas Tree

A pole called the Christmas tree sits between the two racing lanes. It is 20 feet (six meters) ahead of the starting line. There are two rows of red, yellow, and green lights on the tree. There is a row for each car.

The light at the top of the tree is yellow. When it blinks on, the drivers move from the bleach box toward the starting line. A second yellow light flashes when the dragsters reach the line.

The Christmas tree tells the drivers when to get ready and when to go.

Then three more yellow lights flash. These lights warn the drivers to get ready. Sometimes a red light flashes. It means one of the drivers started too soon. That driver is **disqualified**.

When the light turns green, both cars race ahead. The noise is **deafening**. There is an electronic timing board at the far end of the track. It shows the winning time.

By the time two cars have finished their run, two others are in the bleach box, ready for the next heat.

The Timing Tower

The timing tower is a tall building near the starting line. It is between the two racing lanes. From the tower, the race director controls the event. The director makes sure everything runs smoothly.

Timers also work in the tower. Their computers record the cars' speeds. From the tower, the announcer tells the crowd what is happening.

The bleach box is near the tower. When dragsters clean their tires, the vibrations shake

The timing tower is a tall building near the starting line.

the tower. Everyone has to shout to be heard above the noise. Smoke rises in the air, making it hard to see.

Other Workers

There are many workers at a drag strip. Some of them line up the dragsters in the staging lines. They direct drivers to the starting line. They keep an eye on things from the ground.

The track manager and the staff advertise the races. They sell tickets and keep the track and grandstands clean. They help reporters write articles about the races.

Some workers inspect cars. Some pump fuel. Some make sure there are enough hot dogs on hand for hungry fans.

Two Types of Racing

There are two types of drag racing. One is called heads-up racing. In this type, both cars leave the starting line at the same time.

The other type of racing is called bracket racing. In this type of racing, racers receive an

There are many workers and officials at drag races.

average time in **preliminary trials**. This is called a dial-in time.

The dial-in time is written on the windshield with white shoe polish. Drivers try to match their dial-in times during the race. A dial-in time is also called an elapsed time or an e.t.

One driver's time might be slower than another's. The slower driver is given a head start. The faster driver is given a **handicap**. The handicap is the difference between the drivers' times.

Say one racer's dial-in time is 10.00 seconds. Say the other racer has a dial-in time of 9.50 seconds. This means that the first racer will get the green light .50 seconds before the other racer. This makes the race fair.

Top bracket drivers are consistent. They almost always match their average times.

After the Race

The cars are towed to the pits after the race. The driver is given the official race time on a slip of paper.

Cars are towed to the pits after the race.

Race teams compare the time to the driver's other races. They might need to adjust the engine. Repairs might be needed. Then mechanics start working right away to make the car run better.

Chapter 6

A Driver's Life

Top drivers win trophies and cash prizes. They give fans their autographs. Their photos are in racing magazines.

Sponsors

Pro stock cars are expensive. Teams need money for race cars, parts, insurance, transportation, food, lodging, and salaries. Sponsors help the teams pay the high costs of racing.

Sponsors are oil companies, automobile equipment manufacturers, or other businesses.

Sponsors put their logos on the cars.

Sponsor Logo

Racing Slicks

Hood Scoop

Track Official

They put their logos on the cars. Often, a
driver's uniform is covered with sponsor logos.

The best drivers have the most sponsors.
Sometimes the drivers are paid by the sponsors.
Cash prizes might be split between a driver and
a sponsor. Drivers have to do well to keep their
sponsors.

Supporting a winning racer is good
advertising for a business. Sponsors want to be
thought of as the choice of the champions.

The best drivers have the most sponsors.

Then they can sell more of their products to both racers and racing fans.

Life on the Road

Even a top driver's life is not all glory. Sometimes teams have to drive all night to get to the next track. They grow tired of eating fast food and staying in motels.

The team's semitrailer can break down on the road. A car can have engine trouble during a big race. A driver can be eliminated early. But a dedicated team keeps racing.

Not for Professionals Only

Drag racing is not for professionals only. The racing scene attracts semi-pros and amateurs, too. They race because they love the sport.

Many semi-pro and amateur drivers started their careers by visiting local tracks. They read racing magazines. They listened when mechanics talked about how engines work.

The NHRA encourages young people in other ways, too. The association sponsors races, scholarships, and career fairs. It organizes school field trips to racetracks. The NHRA does everything it can do to promote the future of drag racing.

The NHRA encourages young people who want to race dragsters.

Glossary

acceleration—the rate at which something changes speeds

class—separate category for different styles of vehicles

deafening—an extremely loud noise

debris—bits and pieces of litter

disqualify—kick out of a race

handicap—when a disadvantage is put on a racer to make the race more competitive

header—a single pipe that brings two or more pipes together to carry exhaust from the engine

heat—preliminary rounds of a race

hood scoop—a large air duct coming out of the hood of a car

modified—changed to improve performance

pit—area away from the racetrack where mechanics work on vehicles

preliminary trial—another name for heat

production car—car built for sale to the public

roll cage—a strong cage made of steel tubes welded together

safety glass—two pieces of glass fastened with plastic to make shatterproof windshields

sanction—officially approve

traction—the ability of something to grip a surface

wheel base—the distance between the centers of a vehicle's front and rear wheels

To Learn More

Connolly, Maureen. *Dragsters*. Mankato, Minn.: Capstone Press, 1992.

Olney, Ross R. *Modern Drag Racing Superstars*. New York: Dodd, Mead & Co., 1981.

Radlauer, Ed. *Drag Racing*: *Then and Now*. Chicago: Children's Press, 1983.

Smith, Jay. *Drag Racing*. Minneapolis: Capstone Press, 1995.

Sosa, Maria. *Dragsters*. Mankato, Minn.: Crestwood House, 1987.

You can read more about drag racing in *Junior Drag Racer* magazine.

Useful Addresses

Canadian Automobile Sports Clubs
693 Petrolia Road
Downsview, ON M3J 2N6
Canada

Midwest Drag Racing Magazine
3802 Tuttle
Danville, IL 61832

National Hot Rod Association/Jr. Drag Racing League
P.O. Box 5555
Glendora, CA 91740-0950

Popular Hot Rodding Magazine
12100 Wilshire Blvd., Suite 250
Los Angeles, CA 90025

Internet Sites

Drag Racing & Hi Performance Illustrated
http://www.dragracer.com/

Inside Motor Sports
http://www.symweb.com/insidemotorsports/

NHRA Online
http://www.goracing.com/nhra/

Tri 'S' Racing
http://www.cyberhighway.net/~nicks/

Pro stocks go so fast, they need parachutes to slow
down again.

Index

bracket, 31, 32
burnout box, 25, 27

Chevrolet, 13
Christmas tree, 27
Chrysler, 13

Dodge, 13

earplugs, 19

Ford, 13

handicap, 32, 42
headers, 16, 42
heads-up, 31

jaws of life, 22

National Hot Rod
    Association (NHRA), 10,
    23, 40, 45, 46

Parks, Wally, 10
pit crew, 16, 17
pit pass, 17

Plymouth, 13

roll cage, 21, 43

safety crew, 19, 21, 22, 23
safety glass, 21
safety safari, 23
shutdown strip, 21
slicks, 16
sponsors, 35, 38, 40

timing tower, 29
track sweeper, 23